Gutted

Evie Christie

Gutted

Evie Christie

ECW PRESS

MISFIT

Published by ECW Press 2120 Queen Street East, Suite 200, Toronto, Ontario, Canada M4E 1E2

LIBRARY AND ARCHIVES OF CANADA CATALOGUING IN PUBLICATION

Christie, Evie 1979–
Gutted / Evie Christie.
Poems.

"A misFit book".

ISBN 1-55022-710-6
1. Love poetry, Canadian. I. Title.
PS8605.H745G88 2005   C811'.6   C2005-904301-6

Editor: Michael Holmes/a misFit book
Cover and Text Design: Darren Holmes
Cover photo: Evie Christie
Author photo: Aaron Allard
Typesetting: Mary Bowness
Printing: Marc Vielleux Imprimeur

This book is set in Cheltenham and Univers

With the publication of *Gutted* ECW Press acknowledges the generous financial support of the Government of Canada through the Book Publishing Industry Development Program (BPIDP), the Canada Council for the Arts, and the Ontario Arts Council, for our publishing activites.

DISTRIBUTION
CANADA: Jaguar Book Group, 100 Armstrong Avenue, Georgetown, Ontario, L7G 5S4

PRINTED AND BOUND IN CANADA

ECW PRESS
ecwpress.com

Contents

Acknowledgements

Thank you to the Ontario Arts Council for their financial assistance in writing this book.

Aaron Allard, for your imperial leisure. Jonathan Bennett, for the countless hours of work and the mean eye. Lynn Crosbie, for your advice, poetry and otherwise. My editor, Michael Holmes, for your guidance. Nadine James and everyone at ECW for your kindness. Meaghan Strimas, for your own poems (and for having my back), Paul Vermeersch, for your belief in poetry. Gratitude to my family: Caleb Christie, Rachel, Rob and Oliver Christie-Nichols, Karen Christie and Bill Clarke, Mark Christie and Jeanne Brown, Gary and Roslyn Christie (and kids), for being beautiful people. Thanks also to the following teachers, editors and friends for their encouragement: Adam Atkinson, Jennifer Atkinson, Ken Babstock, Chris Banks, Brad Connelly, Adam Getty, Christine Gregory, Adam Hughes, Chad Joyes, Bret Kelsey, Adam Levin, Brendan McCracken, Jake McConnell, Melissa Ormond, Morgan Peachy-Dupon, Emily Pohl-Weary, Tylar Rowely, Conan Tobias, Sarah Walker, Tim Walker, Zach Wells. In loving memory of Katrina Blackbourn and Angela McCarroll.

For my parents,
Karen Christie and Mark Christie

Come and Break My Heart

From your barren cells and basement apartments,
shared accommodations and loveless unions
and not because you mean so much to me.
Come and break my heart because it's rattling and banging,

it's happy candy, this stupid stubborn ruby organ,
this cage-mad bird, the size of an adult fist, knows for once
what it is beating for. And when you said, *At least
we are free*, I didn't tell you, I'm not, I haven't been for years.

I didn't tell you the whole world was water and stone today,
that the ugliest corner of Toronto's west end lit up for me
in pastel Easter cellophane and washed-out fast food hues.
That the bums were more charming than ever, their bottles half

full, their blackened eyes healing amiably, that the seagulls
crooned for me and mattress laden alleys smelled not so much of urine.
No, I think I must've said something about making it home,
or waking up in good time, or rising taxi fares.

New Year's Day Robbery at the Keene
Toronto Dominion Bank

Each of us came together and made a silent prayer that day
to our own individual Gods — yours is much more Old Testament
and spiteful so you tread carefully. Mine is the blazing
open-armed loving Son of God I heard about from my friend's
mom that day I went to Sunday school.
Each of us prayed and wished we'd thought of it first,
slightly sickened by our own menial crimes,
the overwhelming guilt that beckoned
from dresser drawers and closet shelves, in chocolate bars
and nicked cigarettes. But this was it, ski masks, snowmobiles,
the whole shebang. They were found 3 kilometres away,
up the hill past the graveyard, betraying our sombre
hopes, drinking Fifty and losing
half of their loot to their best friend and his wife.

Straw

I've told you about the sheep's heart.
I can't say how many pounds without
The blood, only that it was two fists, mine
Not yours (which are considerably larger).

A man was ablaze on Queen's Park Blvd., we heard
The sirens and later learned on TV that farming is,
As suspected, not the best career choice these days.
It wasn't like that when we smelled of straw.

Remember our sunburnt brothers' bikes,
Funded with eight-hour bailing days, minus lunch?
Or how the smell of shit and feed announced
Formals and final grades? And your first time

In the barn, razor marks straw-lined you
Neck-to-ass, and big, cool bovine eyes, so much
Like the open shutters of heavy German cameras,
You'd sometimes wonder what they kept of you.

I Love Alcoholics

I do, it's not just an eye-catching title.
Their hearts are big and broken,
Preserved in their childhood, their first love
Or some bloody car wreck, preserved
In bourbon, tequila, whatever.
Bruised and bloody, swishing around
In their chest, beating away
To a sad, angry rhythm, and they love
Their mothers and they are so beautiful
When they're drunk that you love them
When they're sober and ugly too.
And they wait patiently for you
To get fed up, for you to leave them,
And if you do they'll love you forever.

The Revival Tent on Highway 7

It took a few weeks for both of us to say how much
we needed it, to be in the sublime thick living forest
of sinners, believers, chatting our confessions
from the rank of the driving unconscious tinny
machinery, moving ever towards work, home,
the dense treeless subdivisions: Polo Court Drives,
Elm Terrace Avenues, babies and bodily fluids sticking
to every shoddy wood panelled or veneered surface.
Their hot and swollen polyestered bodies summoned us
and sure we were sinners in all the ways we wanted to be,
didn't we fuck like wholesome farmers' kids on the hood
of the '89 Pontiac and rob the perpetual doppelgangers
of ex-factory town boys who slept like doped infants
on Christine's low futon? That night we made off
with a killing from the faithful habits of jailbirds,
hockey stars and hairdressers to be. I painted
your cheekbones with copper-tasting blood,
we drove into the night just to feel money
in our pockets and the horror of our exploits.
Or laying low while the cruiser bleeped twice;
the heavy June clotted boots went up the stairs
and down through the back entrance. I had mopped
up all your blood and dressed the wound twice.
They would come again and never believe it was you.
And held up by an old lover, he said he would kill you,
he'd done it before, I talked him down and touched
his forehead with the back of my hand, *I still love you,*
I said, and fixed us all a drink. And they needed us,
our sins more colourful than the fragmented families,
sham marriages or the inevitability of shattered
jawbones and busted teeth. They wanted
our flesh and we were good enough to be pegged
and bled out. They had tickets to heaven
and bingo on Thursday.

In the Cold Months

When university kids return to be
their mother's children, father's names
hang around necks for neighbours to see and say:
how well you've done for yourselves.

And food is served from the rare and hoarded porcelain
of grandmothers — stuffed things, sweet sticky things,
roots. We will migrate blindly towards these bars
over the honky-tonk juke box and karaoke cowboys

we are without obligation, to cities, to speech.
You will ask me about life and lovers, you'll say
what's-her-name is doing well, landed some job
or another, we'll drink the last of our money

and be free, running for your parents' home
or from another chronic brawler, the brute
blood-bombs beating in our chests, until I'm
pressed against the front door frame, words

visible, these times when we believe
in everything, when God and love are as obvious
as the moon, when we scheme against the world
or morning, with all its ugly truth, until next year.

At the Wagon Wheel Saloon and Motel

My friend Lucy calls herself Star — perpetual
schoolgirl (on account of her age and not
dependant in any way upon her attendance record
at Thomas A. Stewart S.S.). On Friday nights
before her shift, we stack the world three or four
lines high, try on wigs and walk four inches
taller than usual, peel back shiny labels
and talk about love and what we'd be doing now.
And hoping she'll get to work on time, we race
down the Hunter Street bridge under what light
the miserly sun allows the moon
until we hit Ashburnham and the first car that stops,
until we surrender her at last to meet
fathers and brothers and lovers for the night.

This is a Picture of Us

Our faces almost looked the same then,
yours more indignant, tongue out in protest, mine
fatter with smiling. I am afraid of black beetles
but we stroke their shiny backs — never kill them

(you hate the noise). I am afraid, but we touch
their backs anyway; in a kitchen in Montreal
you clean fish, barrels of seafood wait
for your thumbs and forefingers, quick and steady,

arms deep in tentacles that cool swollen wrists
and scar tissue. You remember I'm afraid of shellfish too.
Their bent backs and excess legs, like centipedes,
made us shiver, up as close as possible to the buckets

of clicking crabs in Chinatown, slow omniscient
lobsters of Halifax. From Quebec a phone call to remind
me: to set my clock back, to read F. Scott Fitzgerald,
of the politics of language, of biker trials and beetles.

The Bums Out Front of the Scott Mission

I'm just going for fruit usually, but sometimes
I'll walk by for no reason at all. They're not
complacent like the Waverly crowd.

They've got plans, money on horses, ladies to lose, ladies
to get back, dead babies, work boots, a pack of cigarettes,
four bucks, a cot for the night, a friend called Whiskey Carol.

Those bums leaning, wheezing, coughing out front
of the mission have a lot going on. Yesterday's doughnuts,
tomorrow's hangovers, a photograph, letters folded, unfolded

and soft at the edges. Those bums winking, whistling, calling
        out to me,
Hey little girl, made me feel like a million bucks today. I would say
to them, *Were you ever boys?* I would say, *I love you, you bums.*

Our Lady of the A & P

Has no gospel to deliver,
megaphone-less, sign-less, cart-less,
a Botticellian monstrosity.
Head propped, legs crossed, belly bared.
The happiest woman of Bloor Street West,
devoted only to the vendors

of dried fruit and wrapped sandwiches,
outraged only by a lack of fresh
sauerkraut. Takes her time today
in turning, upwelling a bundle of clothing
and Styrofoam containers
to ask, *What's your problem?*

Picking Up My Brother on the Way to Hastings

By the time we get there, Sparky's long gone,
the man of the house is sitting three feet
from the static screen, rabbit ears perched

on a stack of Export cases, one of six ashtrays
in the crook of his elbow, electric heater blazing red,
cigarette (half smoked, stubbed out) tucked behind his ear.

He's only slightly rattled by the jangling
aluminum door, ready with a joke or two,
an offer of Tang and leftover canned spaghetti.

Pull uppa chair, my grandmother was an Ojibwa queen,
I had a shutout that season, some say I woulda made it too,
the NHL, if it weren't for the political climate

and whatnot. I painted Whalen's car last week,
the Germans would be jealous of my attention to detail,
only use the best y'know, it'll pay for the house,

I'm doing it right up this year, you'll see. Yer brother?
That goodfernothin', he smirks, yeah, he's out back
with the young lad doin' God knows what.

Riding County Road 3

There isn't much to be said about crucifix dappled ditches
marking the goalies and promising stars we shared schoolrooms with.

There is talk of new highways and rec centres, the relative health
of fathers — out of rehab, on the wagon, off assistance, in the black.

There isn't much to say of bottles that keep you between blind-drunk
and dazzling, hungry and grave, because you won't allow it.

All the way to room 317 of the Peterborough Regional Health Centre,
holding our breath and wrapping fists in shirt sleeves until we are safe.

My mother is living on atmosphere, her room moves synthetically,
    translucent
tubes and fluids pumping, beating, dripping inside the institutional
    pink organ.

Ruby plastic mugs of milky tea, sweet rhinestone cubes, shiny
cellophane wrap, emerald gelatin and every word here
    has equal value:

lesions and palpitations *down*, birthdays and housework *across*.
Celebrity divorce and tabloid Jesus. God is dead, Elvis lives.

And we will plot against modest cards stabbed
into funeral plants for the phrases you haven't heard today.

Letters Addressed to 745 Palmerston Avenue

You made car seats for a year to get there,
graveyards at the Ajax plant. Not the full
seat, you reminded me often, sometimes just
buckles, for weeks only the pressure of thumbs
against fabric. Between junk mail, final
notices and political pamphlets, I get word
from thousands of miles away.

In September you have a lot to say about
the splendor of the place: Nice, Monaco,
Cannes, a diatribe on the quality of topless
beaches and facts: the tower is leaning alright,
David's got a small dick, it's 25 degrees.
On Sunday we're blowing this popsicle
stand and headed on towards Rome.

If I had a clue where to send it I would write
to you and say: it sounds brilliant,
and warm too. There's not much happening here,
if I were you I'd never come home. I saw your
father, he says he spoke to you, says you're fine.
Tell Andrew I say hello.

In October nothing for weeks, then a postcard
of some Cathedral and half-legible characters:
makes me want to believe in God almost and who
would build a city in the fucking middle
of the water and then wonder why it floods?

I feel like I should write and tell you:
my mom's in hospital and my brother says
the factory's in shutdown. It's bloody freezing
in Ontario but the west is up in flames.

In November, only: I wish I had brought
some beautiful girl and not my buddy
from Friday night hockey. I bought you
a knock-off Rolex for 25 Euros.

In November I wish I could write back:
Remember that year when Charlie fell
into the tree and brought it down in all its spangled
glory? His mother said he'd ruined Christmas.

Livings has got himself a new car, pieced
together from the scrap at Macintyre's auto
wreckers; we put the tin beast right between
two trees. Imagine our luck? When will you be home?

In December a flimsy generic card:
Happy Holidays and your best wishes.
In December I want to write and ask you:
What do I need a bloody watch for anyway?

I Know the Monday Night Women

Half-completed H.R. degrees, one month
pregnant, never fully clothed, *continual becoming
and never being*, women of Monday night strip clubs,
have languorous eyes and luminous asses because
you've told me so. Four a.m. pressed against me as I scratch
bones at the darkness for a cigarette, I am reminded that
Abraham did not sleep his way to fame and neither will you.
All the while I'm thinking of the man below us, how
we sat between leaking taps and guitar picks talking
Jeff Buckley and matching one another can for can,
bottle for bottle, until *Rumours* ended, his mother,
the Chilean climate and a phone call from his son.
I am thinking of him and of my father, of Abraham,
and God and other men I know.

Because I Don't Have a Muse

I rely on cheap drink nights, domestic beer served
four to a bucket. The bartender here has bitten my friend
in a half-assed fight and the trucker to my left knows
every damn secret the Coca-Cola Company holds dear.

There are four or five men waiting to get drunk enough
to say, *Hey little girl, buy you a drink?* And you, drinking
honestly, because Friday night means something after long hot days,
weeks, years. Still poised enough to light a girl's cigarette, willing

to bust up a good working hand on another lousy kid with too much
education and straight shiny teeth, for brief stupid love, for a week
of rain days to lie next to me in bed and coffee and toast, because of this
I will avoid a pissing contest in the alley and maybe the next few.

Door-Buster Sale, Saturday Morning

There is nothing sad about a lineup
waiting for 33 cent turkey dogs on a Saturday morning.

All under five foot five, an amalgam of rolled down
knee highs, all-season overcoats and half-functional umbrellas.

Driven by habit and a prudent understanding of finance,
a hearty competitive drive that renders each limb a weapon

for the last package. Except, says the one in the felt pillbox hat,
that rain is so unkind to particular fabrics,

that paper towels come only in packs of two and that
the Hamburger Helper is fresh out 'til Monday.

Greetings from Barton and Bathurst

There was something you wanted to show me:
I have something I need you to look at, you said. Not the neurosis
of a middle-aged man, arteries clogged stiff with steak and cartilage;
but tarring roofs all day can make a man wonder at the size

and colour of particular spots. A leisurely fear of certain
death — I have timed this out, the lexis that will startle
your features in ways I haven't seen yet. I've counted the syllables
and when the percolator hammers and jolts from within, it will be time.

But now I've gone and tipped the coffee, and now we're onto Kissinger.
Now you've went and apologized and there's a book wrapped in brown
parcel paper, there's a card with an arctic animal — I've seen
      it at *Stanley's*:
the beast in his brutal climate appears to be saying **I'M SORRY**
      in bold caps.

And inside you've written the same, and suddenly nothing is worse
than your boyish love. And tomorrow is Tuesday, tomorrow I'll forget
      the coffee
and I'll remember your terrible fear today when I open this book
      and find the fierce
creature, degraded, useless, saying things in a language he can't
      possibly understand.

Moving to Doc Ford's House

A suicide and ten or so years of ruthless partying
had rendered the place an unwise investment, bad luck, haunted.
My mother pushed and pulled at the soil that year,
digging with her fingers, old soda and pill bottles
    unearthed themselves

for her to rinse beneath our tap until they were shiny enough
to catch light on the window sills. Above the noisy electric wiring
and pipes and floorboards, the voice of a neighbour:
she died of loneliness (and a quantity of sleeping pills),

they didn't find her for three days, in the garden shed there,
she was never quite right. After weeding, the bulbs would need
    to be planted,
the walls scrubbed free of nicotine and the kitchen floor painted
and stickered with coloured diamonds, giving meaning and order
    in their patterns.

Until the Coca-Cola bottles lit up, headlights winked and the truck
    door slammed.
My father sloughing off the possibility of ghosts before going to bed.
Until the staggering sound of words that would keep us awake
    for years,
I'm sorry dear, he doesn't believe in a lot of things.

Sweet Revenge

For years my father tried to tell us about his mother's family,
Saturday evenings in front of the screen — this is Olga at the farm
the slide clicked and we doubted it would jam. These are
    my grandparents,
they would have loved you, they hail from Kingston. We wondered again
how Kingston was supposed to interest us but my father went on.

Flipping black-and-white photographs, letters and sometimes grainy
    film,
driving us to Pembroke, this is the farm, I hid under that tree one year
in a storm, your great-grandfather worked those fields moving stones
every year — like they would ever stop freeing themselves from
    the stubborn dirt.
And still he insists it wasn't enough.

At Christmas my sister will hang the remains of our childhood
on his shabby tree, pointing out the lack of her own early macramé
    or popsicle stick
creations, we will listen to *Sweet Revenge*. My brother will peel a
    tumbler
from the Naugahyde table and push his bottom lip out with his tongue,
skeptical of his own game of 3 Card Monty.

I will think how each cool tungsten image is its own fallacy
of composition, but time's verdict (divorces, bottles, pills,
    blackened eyes,
sanatorium bouts) has got nothing on celluloid. He will call
    from the kitchen,
catching us off guard, What's your Grandmother's middle
    name? Veriole,
I know it's Veriole. But I'll let him start again.

Nig, Son of Debbie

Through the Hiawatha brush we made headway, promises.
With each turtle liberated and pointed back towards the beach,
in mouthfuls of Ojibwa curses and nostrils surging smoke,
we would at least finish high school.

Years later you found out, exposed me: malevolent, brutal, white
in pages from your grandma's book, clippings from *Maclean's*
and the *Toronto Star*. My defense was a plastic bag jingling
with brown bottles for the walk. My defense

was that I have no history, a secret mythology of corn roasts
and Tupperware, sitcoms and house pets. My dad may be a Jew
and my mom a Gypsy nomad and besides I don't care. *That's
     even worse,*
you said, and grabbed a fistful of Deb's cigarettes for the trip.

I'm Thinking About Memphis

About the brand of cigarette you were smoking when you wrote
from Virginia, the ashes that collapsed gently into the crease of your
words, the washed-out sketches, watermarks, of waterfalls, state Capitol
buildings, a bird or statue I will never see. It seems that all we write about
these days is love, though neither of us knows it anymore: mine wasted
in silence and bottles, yours a devoted enemy. I never knew how much
I relied upon your ruthless faith to disturb my staunch egoism,
my ugly heart now beating only because it knows no other way.
I am thinking about Memphis, its squat and desolate strip-mall bars,
the man who traced for you the map and penned a crude blue route
    to Texas.
Did he smell like your past lover, or were you imagining it, do all men
on the road to New Mexico grin crooked grins and smell of tobacco
and printing inks, desert their woman for the splendid ache of youth
and return each night to remind her of their absence?

Slaughterhouse Sonnet

A million smiling Isaacs before you
Stab cherry coin slots into the thick pink collars.
Those who refuse to die, those who twitch, who,
With bloated eye and rancid hoof, take their time
In dying, will of course be shot in the face.
When you've been here as long as you've been,
They give you the company stopwatch:
Chain link vest, glove, glove, coveralls, light
Jog to station B and a piss takes 15 minutes,
Anything beyond and you're docked. Don't even
Think about a quick jerk for Christ sake, do it
On lunch or on the fucking drive in and you
Know for damn sure there's a God who's given such
Glorious freedom, endless vistas of blood and bone.

The Properties of Loss

In the American Midwest last week tornadoes
gave proper endings to so many trailers
and porches and bikes; somewhere a bus litters
appendages on a hot dusty street, but this new death
leaves us barren. Synthetic lawn chairs and Plexiglas
signs separate smoking sections, tiger lilies mark
the gravelly attempts at decorum in these strip-mall
healthcare centres, Styrofoam cups keep vigil and loss
is demoralized, leaving only the bloodless remains
of unopened sandwich meat and overdue bills in your name.

There is a Place in Trois Rivières

Where sweet boozy drinks are served in synthetic
coconuts, pineapples, to sweet boozy girls
and each waitress is the kind you'd
give anything to fuck — I know this

to be truth. There is a beach just outside,
not so far, where glass concedes to rock and tide
and acts gentle now, even lovely, for the beating. 100
yards away Jesus' eyes are bleeding on a woman's

front lawn and I'm wondering how he hung like
that for so long, how strong the pegs, and why didn't
he give, tear from the rancid planks, what with the weight
and all. And there are things I do know: you'd give

your right arm for the waitress I guess, and I'd like
to know how a girl could be so livid without even a drop
of blood to spoil the shadow from her eye, and I'd like one more
drink, maybe something with a sword and a cherry.

They've Gone and Sealed the Gates to Heaven

They've moved in without notice, a tireless
brigade of progeny, dogs, SUVs and turtle-
shell glasses. Our wasted youth means
nothing now, shameful etchings and the bones

of our habits. We won't be together again
in the famous grotto of this city's rusted
underbelly and only rumours of ex–factory town
violence to swell in the throats of those we left

behind to dig the tunnels and fasten the wires of life-
style, for affluent babies, mute in their glorious
nothingness and fathers, jingling ice in high-
balls saying things like *Christ, for the cost of this place.*

Rickety wives who'd make you believe in immaculate
anything and know what it is to seal the parched
cavities of ache, the places you became each
other, where your boyfriend stuck two fingers
in your friend and smoked you up a million times

and once Dawn bled there for an hour before the stars
cleared from your lidded eyes and you wondered at broken
glass until you wrapped a shirt sleeve around her
ankle and talked about the burning time
of particular paper and she tongued at the spaces

in your mouth, where the dentist had been, his elbows
grazed your nipples and now this city's gone to hell:
the bridges are wedged, slabs of granite clot the mausoleum
doors and even the heavens forget, you've been told,
but you can smell the new paint from a hundred miles away.

An Honest Woman
— for Meaghan

As stubborn as any man
you tell me you've settled for smoking
and argue further that while your lover
is gone you've regained a closeness
with a certain typewriter
and shun the men scratching at your door
for *Finkleman's 45s* and maybe a white vermouth or two.

And I've told you that women don't drink vermouth
anymore and of course you say:
Look, Evie, no man is crazy enough
to marry you, and you're likely
barren and also a cold-hearted bitch at times,
best suited to pornography and affairs
with men who need anything but love.
What you lack in all other facets of life,
at least, for the very least, you could make up for
in shutting the fuck up and just having a drink
and listening to the music for once.

Your Wife

I've yet to meet her in person
but the photographs have me
curious, the backdrop hardly
worth noticing, in fact I didn't
notice how the universe retreated
into the dark boundaries of the frame.

The way the whole day must
have smelled of cut things,
stems, leaves, grass, how the trees
must have bowed into her easy
light, bashful when confronted
with her staggering way.

I've been standing on this
balcony, never six feet from
my sins, I've been leaving windows
and doors open for your scent
to withdraw itself from the linen
long after you've gone.

I've been meaning to ask you
what did that day smell like
and did you take hold of her hand
and dance until her sundress swelled above
the birthmark on her thigh, and what
did you say when you got in this morning.

Love and Mortgages

Some lousy kid messing up your place,
your head, drinking up all your beer
and spending your hours, your money
on taxi rides and stockings.

Until one comes along with a career
and curled eyelashes, a driver's licence
and her own wristwatch, with a belly for babies
and later some comfortable devotion.

She'd never fill her days with sleep
and smoke and she knows the importance
of a dollar and all about what it takes
to be in love and buy a house.

Domestic Byzantium

I'm not stalling, I just know all progress
leads to death. The television news broadcasts
the mathematical impossibility of life, in rocket ships
and car rides through the country and housewives
who reach precision in the household Mecca of labelled
canisters, Tupperware separated from lids in drawers,
laundry pulled, pressed, stacked, reaching permanence
in the finality of 22s, 44s or the dependable .357,
brain matter and bone fragments exploding through pale
Bonne Bell features, not waiting to use provided orifices.
Teeth in twos, still attached to gum and bits of hair and scalp
make their way up and expand physical identity, make relics
of bodily existence in a domestic Byzantium
of Avon necklace charms and rhinestone hairpins.

If Things Had Been Different

Yesterday would have been a chamber
of opened things. We would smooth out
newspaper on the floor of an unclothed room,
liberate lunch from waxed paper sheets
and later drag boxes from the doorway.
One would hold the glass bird we found
in Chinatown and we wouldn't think to look
for the photographs just then or wonder why
our letters were stacked like paper trophies
on our nightstands. We would be tired
from the sandwiches and unpacking and we'd
want to rest again and finish tomorrow.

Every Time a Lover Asks *How Could This Happen?*

Remind them that packing up your green sweater,
three pairs of shoes, super absorbency tampons,
two party dresses and one third
of the albums leaning in the crate by the TV stand

is nothing spectacular. Tell them: there are people in your lifetime
who've eaten human hearts, and not for want of food,
and a thousand dirty wars later the news anchor
with the orange tan and perfect arching brows has found

a healthy microwaveable diet she'd like to share,
that you laughed so hard when your friend's boyfriend bound
your ankles and wrists in metallic duct tape,
that you pissed yourself and the tape would not bind your lips
        for the saliva.

That the Leafs have not won the Cup since 1967 and every year
your neighbour says this is the year. That there are one hundred
        and fifty
Toronto poets trying to find meaning in the abrupt filthy light
        of the Don
between Broadview and Castle Frank each day.

Eulogy Girls

*God is in the midst of her, she shall not be moved; God shall
help her, at the approach of morning.* Psalms 46: 2–11

Some of them believe in heaven and hell,
the bumbling, gurgling eulogy girls — anaesthetized
until they can almost feel the burning white
halos of love flirting with their hair.

And what does it take to see God, to be with God,
to be his girl and lay against his chest?
First you must bring yourself close, close enough
to see him, almost, line your nostrils

until sparkling rhinestones form at the edges, sleep,
don't wake up for the muffled voices or fingers
digging past hipbones into pockets
for change or matchbooks, turn a light cerulean,

turn to face him, azure knuckles, sapphire lips,
open your eyes. It takes something like this,
or driving fast, fires, misfires, heavy currents,
light cigarettes, for those girls to call you an angel too.

Hearing From Jennifer

It would take me a half hour of small talk,
weddings, mortgages, adulteries and garden tips
to get to you. And why not, haven't I carried
your confessions for years? Your cock-eyed love,
your half-assed crimes. I've been waiting for word,
to know which habit has whitewashed you at last.

And now when I'm expecting so much, only
a few petty headlines, a collapse, pharmaceuticals?
She thinks for a while, exhales, no, amphetamines.
I would write to you, phone you, wake you
in your mother's basement and beg for a cigarette
(I'm lousy at rolling). Sit with you on the border

of the buzzing, beating, battered Reserve
and talk you down from your terrible bliss.
I love you, Christ knows I love you enough
to be there when they drain you and pump
the clean formaldehyde through your corrupt
channels, it will grip my throat and arrest

my stupid heart. I would dig for you, unearth
you, lie with you like Isis, piece you together,
a Picasso jigsaw, fuck you until I'm sure you're
dead, lick the blood from between
my fingers, where it sticks and pulls
and hurts you no more.

Porn Stars and Pharmaceuticals

When the air gets too heavy to hold up our limbs,
to speak, to fuck, neither of us can get up to turn it off.

Concerned with issues of gravity, reminding oneself to breathe,
the itch behind your knee you won't get to before it's gone.

When the nausea relents there are hours of silence, immobility,
to look forward to. You say your body is soft buckskin, but I am

all eyes, eyelashes, eyelids, I am all consciousness and I wonder
how you continue to light our cigarettes and who is doing
      the delicate work

of keeping us alive. We are looking to her for a common focus,
the bronze goddess on the screen, her agility, her aloof acrobatic

approach to love, we agree she should win some type of award,
a medal perhaps. Not only for the obvious flexibility

but for the obvious flexibility and the quantity of mammary-like
substance, jiggle-less, astounding! The ingenious use of each orifice,

the harsh inflections in each submissive syllable. We agree
she is Eastern European, that she is the best at what she does,

that people should be talking about her and the wonderful things
      she's doing.
I am thinking of inertia, I am thinking that lovelessness needn't
      be mute,

that shackles don't have to be cheap metaphors, they could be
glossy and fuchsia, that we should fuck until we are raw and bleeding,

be magnificent in destruction, use each orifice as though it were
the proper one, and of just how much I owe to Rita Faltoyano.

Things My Psychiatrist Would Say About Me

And I'd like him to speak on my behalf, that sober voice
Cracking out an elegy or best wishes on some special day.

To give those grand apologies you'd never take from me and all of you
Would assemble and listen to this rational man and feel like

You understand, for just a moment, why, when he says:
She's twenty minutes late if she shows up at all, commitment issues

(To anyone but herself), never takes her shoes off, sleeps in, drinks
    too much,
Stands me up, answers my phone, talks to my wife, has a great ass,
    she doesn't mean it,

Really, she loves you. It will be in the way he says it, authoritatively, behind
An Expansive Cherry desk. You will feel his breath on exposed parts, thighs,
    shoulder blades.

You will listen to him and believe the hell out of everything he says because
He reminds you of your stern fathers or the creepy married-in uncle,

Or the doctor who slipped it in first (without the glove) and winked.
And your fingers will trace the grain lines of his desk before you head off

And they will smell of polish for days and you will understand at once why
I need all this, you will even think about sleeping in and showing up
    late tomorrow.

Lady Like You

I would give it all up if I could
for quiet patience and a baby or two,
sleep at night because it's sensible
and wake for another day of monotony.

But your early days disturb your ocean eyes,
I've seen them blackened with love and gin,
I've heard your girlish whimper
though you swore it was a growl.

Your blood-slick knuckles beating softly,
not sure anymore about the decency of survival.
Legs pinched together against buzzing schoolroom
busy-bodies, ears hot and ringing since breakfast.

But now that we're here there's no reason
we shouldn't make use of our cruel youth,
pry whiskey from these puerile married men
with schoolgirl wonder, stockings and collarbones.

Lady, like you, I'm here to get vile,
to know what it is a sinner feels,
to wake up alone, corrupt and queasy,
make promises to God we can't possibly keep.

Alphonse and the Egg
— for Aaron

A damp slap of wing from my balcony.
We are here in the mornings, together
These days. For weeks you collected twigs
And cardboard and for weeks

I swept it all away — a cleaner sort of look,
For company I guess. You came
From that thicket of skyscrapers each day
Until you were done.

Yesterday this small pale egg
Was a nuisance. I thought about
Nudging it with my flip-flopped foot
Over the edge, rolling it into nothingness.

I closed my eyes against the grey Bloor
Morning, café-curries and stir-fry below,
The beginnings of the hot-dog-cart's thick
Grease-heat, all twisting my gut.

Or was it you, perched above it all, something
So grotesque, so instinctive, I knew you had come
Some distance. Your stance, it smacks of faith
And love and, well, it just reminds me of home.

Women of Tuesday Nights

I want to lie for you like a centrefold
Just like the women of Tuesday nights.
Every man will have such a woman,
Even yours. I might be his one day,

(It could be Wednesdays or Fridays).
He will pick up racketball or maybe
Rekindle his love for Modern Hebrew
And he'll smell better and fuck better.

Don't worry, lady, he doesn't fancy me
Any better or more, see I'm bony in places
And haven't any tits to speak of. But I like
The way my name rolls off his tongue,

And how he calls me kid and baby
And says, *Well, well, look at you.*

My Father Could Drive for Hours

Without so much as a word as to where we were
going. We collected shotgun shells, in K-Way
pockets, in Nephton, the mining town

where he was raised. Bright elementary
coloured tubes we found more valuable than mica,
the six-inch cylinders cut from the rock for dynamite

blasts, or the sapphire quarries filled with rain water. His
landscape was the Canadian Shield, its granite hills, the Warsaw Caves,
the Petroglyphs, the Jack Rabbit Trail, Percé Rock, Gaspé

Peninsula, he was tireless, until sick at our indolence,
he drove us home, quieter than ever. Our heads charged, electric,
with synthetic earphones, forgetting as fast as we could.

Folding Clothes

Pulling wooden pegs off stiff white T-shirts,
everything smells clean and cheap somehow,
like bleach, and my face is hot because I believe
everyone passing is looking, knows, that I wash
my clothing in the bathtub — and yours too. I fold
laundry to the afternoon news, lottery numbers
and car wrecks. I scrub and brush and polish
to *Nashville Skyline* and later *Nighthawks at the Diner*
and I'm hungry for breakfast all day. I have seven dollars
for groceries and three hours to look pretty and cook dinner,
set out dishes, make the bed and forget what you said
about all of the things we will do when we have money
and time, and remember to run my fingers
along the window sills and tend to the geraniums.

Some of the Secrets I've Kept

At the Damascus Gate in some bloody riot or another, I bent low
into the taxi while you spoke throatfulls of broken Hebrew
and glass, bent low until my hair was well-smelled,
my panties grazed with some soldier's trigger finger.

And hitching to Beersheba from the Dead Sea my legs
slack and promising in the rearview mirror as you argued
politics and smoked the driver's Lucky Strikes until
the desert offered tea and gasoline from its voluptuous hills.

Or on the Greyhound along St. Laurent Blvd. in the snowstorm,
after makeshift trailer home church and Christmas light crucifixes,
after half-lit messages of Jesus' love all the way to Highway 7,
I wondered if I could go it alone, or with Jesus —

the stout dark Israelite or the sandy blue-eyed saviour.
Would my youth be enough for him? Would he trade it all
for some shifty kid with smooth shoulder blades, forgive it all
on the promise of more? Would you break his nose if you knew?

A List I Found in your Fannie Farmer Cookbook

On the back of a red Craven A pack, torn at the edges,
a perfect rectangle, holding a page for you for years.

But you've been busy, a career, divorce and babies that grew
slowly emptied out of your rooms, silenced hallways

and uncluttered kitchen tables. Half of the records, photographs,
half of everything gone. It looks different but it smells the same,

tea and lavender, Spanish women depicted on tins of powder
(the scents I imagine and seek out when I'm far from you).

My hands move instinctively over ledges into books
of photographs and poetry and I try to imagine the woman

my age (maybe) with babies and friends who would change
or waste away and die a thousand miles from here. Her hair

tied back, planning days that smelled like this. Fold
the laundry, pick up milk, pay heat bill, paint nails, water plants.

Carpenters' Wives

Thinking he'd better be dead, or at least
smell of something that gives you the right,
I would say, go to sleep, there are only two places
around here he could be anyway.
But when he comes in, boards creaking
beneath work boots, his trumpets, leaving
the ruins of Friday night pay on the counter,
and matchbooks and billiard winnings, a pint glass
you'll return to Luscious Linda's or the Legion
in the morning, you'll let your small ribcages
and dimpled thighs give under the brutish love
and weight of bourbon-bellied men, beneath
a hundred promises, not one of which is sleep,
and forget each of your violent aspirations until morning.

Beyond Douro County Lines

Somewhere beyond Douro County lines,
possibly County Road 3, my father
moves inside a well-lit kitchen, peeling
squash or singing a song nobody knows
anymore. I can see the scene take form
from the drive: he will stoop for the onions
in the bottom cupboard and graze
his lover's ass nonchalantly, as if grazing
an ass were as obvious as breathing
for an old man. But I don't need to look,
I just know these things now.

I need to look at the sprawling maple,
the woodpecker's life's work in infinite
holes and holes I can't see yet for the time
of night. Has it always been there?
And you'd be wrong to think I don't need
to look up, I don't believe those stars
were there before, prove to me that one's
not blinking for me, prove to me
that one was there last night, when I was
still thinking twice about this and you
and how easy it is to travel back in time.

When I step inside, the door will take its time
whining shut, my father will rest against
the counter and catch his breath, from the singing
or the upward motion, and he won't see me
there just then, he'll pat his chest and wink
at his girl, too at ease with his impending
casualty. June bugs will buzz and glisten between
screen panels, busying themselves before
imminent death, and the whole world will
glint and shift around me and I'll try my best
to stand completely still, hoping it won't notice me.

My Best Friends' Mothers

Were all coffee and plates of eggs, balanced
inside elbows — orange-coloured drinks pass to the right,
and in the morning hair down from awesome heights
(girded sternly by bobby pins and banana clips).

Toast cut sideways, permission slip on fridge, clothes laid out.
Some days my mother rocked methodically in a chair upstairs smoking
and forgetting the turkey that never thawed on Christmas day,
or the man at the butcher shop who put ground beef wrapped in paper

in her school bag — *Something for your belly,* he winked. And other days,
hair restrained in the gilded Spanish barrettes, picking strawberries,
moving swiftly in the rows with a baby on her hip, planting bulbs,
pulling weeds, folding, pressing and coffee and juice and eggs.

July is for the Rich

Garbage piles around Spadina corners: a fat black slug,
a natural border between those who do and those who don't
have to know little boys who drown in rec centre pools, that summer
parades are for the brown, black and burdened and the east
    is congested

with mothers, dreaming derelict dreams of Popsicle stained
babies, water fountains and washed-out Polaroids. Intimacy is not
optional here, it tugs and pulls at sleeves, it sticks and sucks
palms, it strains and hurts to remember its piercing

imperfections. The bohemian/ intellectual/ socialist/ activists
slouch and prowl College Street bars, smoke French cigarettes,
wish they were thin enough to be artistic: it's fun to look poor.
In Yorkville a slick black Jaguar sleeps, its mistress eats heavy foods

inside a yellow stucco building, adjusts thousands of dollars
    of mammary-
like substance and picks at white teeth. July is for the rich
    who'll never
drink cheap beer in swollen bars, watch wet quarters queuing
patiently on pool table borders or stick to a lover thigh to hip.

Riding with Old Irv

In the rattling domestic pickup we fly
over the Grand River and make our way
back from the Nanticoke hydro plant,
leaving behind the stench of Lake Erie
and a nine-hour union day. Another meeting
full of men with thick blistered fingers
and a truckload of one liners, lamenting
the loss of smoking rights as they drink
cans of beer slyly from foam slipcovers.

This is the gal they've got doing the papers
come Monday, can you's give her a hand?
My body flinches at the barrage
of clever retorts to follow:
I'll give her both, I'd give my right arm.
And at the thought of Irv, removing his palm
from my thigh (because I reminded him of his
daughter) and all the lust I felt beneath the
comfortable weight of his coal-digging palm.

At Big Ross's in the Summertime

Mismatched yellowing letters hang soberly,
promising staples: bread, milk, cigarettes
and fireworks, gasoline and worms. And the local kids
cool their backs against the concrete arena, smoke
by the creek or make out in the graveyard.
And the bonspiels are over, hockey gives way to slow pitch,
men drink beers against trucks, leaning endlessly
into the evening and the women at the church bazaar talking pies
and other women. The only thing that will interrupt
it all will be the big barbeque, a car wreck, the craft show,
a drowning, babies, and now moving restlessly
down Harbord I'm promising always to come back,
get on the Greyhound and wake up there, sit on your porch like
I had nothing to do, kneel in your garden and dig myself out.

I Found this Eviction Notice

One of the twelve you snatched
off the door of our place on London Street
that year, and lighting a cigarette said,
Who would do a thing like that?

And marching down to the Peterborough County courthouse
with a violation or two in your fist, you had the JP
at your mercy, candy fuchsia nails and borrowed dress,
I imagine you said something like, *Who would do a thing like that?*

I Don't Know, It May Just Be the Weather

Mix of sun and clouds, but as humid
as I can remember it ever being,
and I'm scared, this country is changing,
even here where it's been like this forever.
I felt alright though when the guy with the
Kiss My Bass foam mesh hat asked me,
Anywhere we can buy beer around here?
And my chest is tight, my limbs grow
heavy when I hear the gas pumps are gone
and the neighbours are divorced.
Bastards, I needed this, all of it,
to feel sane again. But I'm sure they needed
me at some time too, not to wake up
drunk in Toronto with you,
smoke a cigarette and go back to sleep.
They needed me to go to school and look beautiful
so they could continue to bake pies,
play bingo and talk about people
like us. So at night they could put rollers
in their hair and drink a beer with Letterman
and, Fridays, drink a few beers.
And now I know I should have told them
I'd be home sometime, everything
will be okay for all of us,
Nothing needs to change, I would have said.

I'm Breaking My Heart

Because it smells like this, and hurts a bit with cold,
and fall is always the same. Fall's always the same,
the way it drops and bleeds red and orange
pumpkins and sour apples, short-lived
(so we can already see their destiny
in carved-out bodies, in mottled streets and baked pies).
And here, where it draws like magnet force
sad bodies and bottles close to corners,
vents and doorways, and here, three days later
than was advisable, I wake up, unmade bed,
pillowless, hurting. And I've tried beer
and poetry, mystery after mystery
and you and you and you, phone calls, photographs,
letters home. *Wake up*, you say, *and eat soda crackers,*
outside it's fall, it's falling. Inside though there's sleep
in this tomb on Bloor Street and memories
of anticipating hockey rinks stained red and blue
in careful stripes and circles, crystallized snowbanks,
kamikaze graveyard toboggan rides and chapped familiar
faces I hardly see anymore. Inside it's dreams for days.

Old Men Sitting in Dizengoff Square at Night

Or Christie Pits in the blackout, don't worry
about weather patterns, the price of gasoline
or leaks that sing their poverty
from ceiling tiles and faucets. They don't
think about lumps in the breast that spread
and degraded the women who wrapped
their sandwiches for work or war and swollen
with babies broke ceramic mugs not so far
from their dinner seats. They eat radishes
and apples, drink homemade wine
and remind me that it's absurd to dream about
the shallow grave we placed the robin in that summer,
beneath leaves and damp grass until rain exposed us
in the tiny bones and soft matted feathers.

Not a Love Poem

When you call tonight from that sensible country
Do try and remember the time difference.
Consider I may have resolved my insomnia
Or taken pills that do the trick.

Believe for a moment I may be in love
With a young man I met at a party in Parkdale.
He wore a tie that I touched and noticed aloud, even
Said, *Hey, that's a nice tie* — it started there.

And wonder if maybe I never got that letter
Or the picture of you tanned and grinning, like the sun
Was your lover and that land wasn't settled,
And so it tilted in for you alone to scythe and bear.

We were born two days apart in another irrelevant city,
Our mothers told us of each other's cheap pilled robes
And scarring, stretch marks mapping isolation, and how
Their young landscape, degraded, was a better dream.

And remember, old friend, though we weren't born to be
Lovers, we were born together, naked and bloody, into April.
And know that I'm awake, the clocks set ahead or back, waiting
To hear happy birthday or I miss you something terrible.

That We Could Let the Season Fall

Not so long ago your parents loaded
you into the yellow Dodge — a meteor
shower made you forget
just how much you hated your sister. The rusted flatbed,

the smell of gasoline and blackness
were a universe. These days you are never
far from pills that keep you three feet
from anywhere, half a mile between thought and speech,

and your mother calls too often for even
you to believe it's okay — believe
there is a universe, stars ablaze and falling,
burning, settling into darkness. That we could let the season fall

around us without recalling the times
we smiled artlessly at the buckled skies
would be mad. Let the scar
beneath your chin remember a hostile winter, a BMX

and flying, books studded with bus tickets,
ash smudged verses, your fervent youth.
Let a voice remind, across cities tonight,
how you hitched Highway 7, out of your village, .357 replica

tucked in your waistband, to meet the world half
way. Now there are cigarettes and weak syndicated
TV, now there is instant coffee, blinds drawn
and a phone that sings from that world you cannot bear to answer.

Twenty-Fifth Birthday Suit

I woke up that way and rolled back over searching
for the signs and still my breasts are small and standoffish,
no signs of commitment, of children or lovers lining my hips.
But my left hand curves inward where shards of glass confounded
the best plastic surgeon my parents could come by, my sister's grit
imbeds itself forever here and my crooked teeth bear my father's lapse
in peripheral judgment — left a knick in the highboy and my mother
bawled for the tongue she imagined lost forever with the cat's eye
marbles and foreign coins in my belly. The rest comes down to
personal miscalculations: the BMX-ed chin, the haymaker-ed nose,
the hemorrhaging heart, cured, in whatever's been cheap or free
for the evening. And I am twenty-five and nothing could prepare me
to hear about Roger Nielson's merciless cells — they will remember
him today. Didn't I tell you all that season how great he'd been looking,
how I was sure he'd been on vacation, in love, working out, maybe even
given up on red meat? Even when that kid on the Greyhound
        told me he
was ready to assemble by the bed and chat his goodbyes
        from the stratum
of standby stars, un-gowned, broad featured, hockey jersey boys,
and all my love is corrupted into these throbbing feverish acts of faith
        — and you've not
been drinking for nine days, you say, come home and it will all
        be different, your bones
are aching and half of the albums are missing, half of everything
        is nothing.

Reckoning a Different Kind of Love

Not love at all really, but I spent hours
and months drinking gin or beer on your balcony
into daybreak. I wouldn't tell you how your posture
and stride reminded me of my father's, or the cool,
ritual way a heart can beat, knowing what is not right,
what it doesn't want, and beat again.

And still I dream of you, when I'm not dreaming
of the years of my life spent watching
the Trent Severn Waterway from the stern
of a pontoon boat, from the hydraulic lift lock above
the embankment, the courthouse, war-time bungalows,
a carnage of derelict factories and rust-pitted El Caminos,

hoping soda cans and gasoline eddies would barter
themselves for some other, shining world.
And economical dreams, limbs flailing
from the bridge into Squirrel Creek, my brother knew
what it was to fly, and I knew what it was to feel
each organ relent to such inborn freedom and rejoice.

You cannot know these hands — how they've sliced
through bait with a toothed hook, hauled a line, smacked carp
against rudder, how they wanted to be other, for you:
clean, white palms that have never known blood,
or how I'd start from sleep to your easy love
and offer water and stone for your trouble.

Love Me and I'll Love You

Love me like you never had a mother.
Or, love me like you loved that girl
From Jackson — was it Raphael?

And did she say, *Ooh I love the way
That tastes*, or was that another
Man's girl I'm remembering now?

Love me this way and I'll do the same
Right back; see I'd like it to be vile
Just like being clocked in the face,

Oh! And also like candied cherry licked
From palms and we could have bloody sweet
Broken toothed smiles to show for it.

Love me like your wife was never
Coming home or like we were dying
And had only this one day to do it all,

We could finish each other off before
The end and later watch TV and drink
Colas in bed and grin and say,

We shouldn't do it again — I'll be out
By six, before her car hits the freeway
(And there's usually gridlock anyway).

Sandstorm on College Street

Yes, there was a sandstorm on College Street
today. They were digging up a system
of pipes and organs at a calm union pace,
leaning against shovels and backhoes

like surgeons who had opened my grandfather's
chest, saying things like: *What the fuck do we do with this?*
One was carrying a plank, gloriously, above his shoulders,
not bothering to wipe the stinging sweat from his eyes

and men in suits loosening their ties looked
up and away, their horrible freedom too much.
And of course I thought of you, not the weighted belt
that held the mystery of your days, in nails, the Estwing

and die-cast bolts, your resigned joy when the rain came
hard, but you far away and young in the sand — we walked
the beach for days like ambassadors of youth, being strong
and beautiful and stupid against headlines of artillery fire,

and I looked away too, not knowing how much I would
forget and the way love would squander itself in these small
and brilliant moments neither of us recalls anymore. The way
love gets buried and we mistake its freedom for labour and sweat.

Zombie Love (Haikus)

The last time I see
A zombie movie we still
Act like we're in love.

Not all zombies eat
Brains you know — I bet that some
Like cherry cola.

Take Philosophy
Get really profound, there are
Zombies everywhere!

We see the Haitian
Zombie film, I cry because
They are slaves. You laugh.

There is nothing small,
Fine or Japanese, just beer
And you and the films.

You know I have to
Write zombie poems and say,
Remember that night?

We get together,
Night of the Living Dead, but
That's it, right, no moves.

I'm annoyed that you
Don't like *Zombie High*, even
For the fact it's dire.

You have sex with her,
Take 40 pills and sleep it
Off — wake up refreshed.

My love has my heart
In a jar, he is sick and
Of course I love him.

My love has a hand
On my neck, I walk straighter
This way — good zombie.

When will he eat my
Brain or is he one who likes
Hearts and colas more?

I can't remember
Who is the zombie now, who
To fear — could be both.

After *White Zombie*
I know I love Lugosi
As much as you do.

You say you'd like to
Kill a man before you die,
But not with voodoo.

Or a woman, you
Say, *No a girl, who'd call you
A woman?* And laugh.

Tonight I dream them
At my doors, crying for me.
I am one of them.

We find zombie porn:
I think he wants to pop her
Cherry blossom, wink.

Don't fuck to zombie
Porn, you cross the necro line,
You feel dark after.

Don't fall in love with
A zombie, he will eat your
Brains, steal your cola.

13 More Reasons I'm Single

You may still love me.
And this is why you've been drinking for twenty days straight.

The fall comes and apples remind us
of sex and sleep.

You call to say you're stepping it up,
off red meat,
on to better things,
haven't thought of me in weeks.

Break a window and tell me
you've changed.
Tell the cop to mind his own fucking business.

Write from New Orleans
of one-night stands and beads you've sent me.

Confess you understand those who've wanted
to break my neck.

Date a capitalist, a lawyer,
a corporate lawyer.

Leave her saying there are girls
and there will be girls.

Break my heart and feel like
we're even.

Drop off a Christmas present.
Note the length of my hair.

Recall the times we ate only apples
for lack of money and tell me you've had better sex since.

Move on to better things again.
Try a liver cleanse.

Drunk-dial to say
you don't know why I'm not picking up.

Before the Cosmic Darkness of Warehouses

You lived in the here and now between
church hall meeting coffee, flimsy
red Naugahyde-bound bibles
and benders: fists thumping
the bar, band doing another AC/DC
at your request, man the world
was yours, on fire, brilliant.

There was the aching bloody
heart of the man, the wiry electric
energy that carried us above
your head of clean hair, blue jeans,
brown suede jacket with fringes
(there is no man who cleans up like
you the day after)

and into your arms — nothing
could stop us from running
at you or gripping the throttle
on the old Honda or saying
we wanted to be desperados.
And against it all, your voice, ten
years later from the telephone

booth inside Kingston
Detoxification Centre, dragging
God and love into it all when you
know damn well God knows nothing
of bottles and syringes that draw you
ever away from the world and into
the pink — that's the other guy.

Legs Up to Here

There is a man singing hallelujahs
tonight, into a CB radio: *Jesus
has come my brothers!*

And let's not pretend we're not dying
to know what a shanty town might
look like, smashed to shit, on fire,

unhinged. Of course we didn't actually pray
to see, for ourselves, just this once,
how wind and a bike-chain negotiate

the limbs off an obese waitress, peg
an infant to a garden shed. A million
miles away we know a girl is dead,

there is a suitcase, there are digits — and who
needs dental records when we've got a torso
that fits? Does the cosmos register such

triumph, remember where it's hidden
the pieces? Will we wake up one day knee deep
in arms and legs, for mothers to kneel and say, *at last?*

Visiting My Village

The lethargy of heat has the whole place moving
in a sham of action and progress, humming
with lawn tractors, fire truck engines, whirring
and stalling into another drunken evening
of tune-ups, kids calling shotgun in the borrowed
vehicles of step-parents, heroic in pursuit before
the whining sirens get close and the cop winks
and says, *Bring it home boys, you should be ashamed.*

The amour of the cicada rests halfway down
my mother's oak tree and I remember the man
I didn't love, how we lay beside one another until
spring gave way to summer, held up in the second
floor of the rooming house on Ben Yehuda.
Telling me stories of his six years as a soldier,
his wife and the baby he might've acknowledged
before he knew other things, his first gun buried
in his father's backyard (the second on the bedside table).

Startled at my lack of ambition, and my age,
rising early and finding day labour to prove
our differences, resentful of the men I read, jealous
of my lazy youth, feigning rancour and buying fabric
for my ceiling. Telling me I could do with some order,
time in service, that killing a man was about necessity
and not passion, that work is what brings value to our time
and buys me the things I love. That he'd be crazy
to stick around for unseemly lust and sliced fruit
in the morning, and that he'd like me to get up and fix
a real breakfast tomorrow before noon.

Gutted

On a sacred native burial ground in central Ontario,
a campground staked its place, in tents
and trailers and the fishing huts. Fat kids
from Ohio drank beer from cans and built fires.

None of the locals would eat a thing
out of that lake. One bucket for guts, scissors, two
knives, one bucket for heads.
There are accepted ways to clean a fish.

But we're just here to smoke. Metallic green and blue
scales shimmer and we're satisfied with the order.
A gutted fish is the product of a series of movements:
hook slips, belly plundered, bones lifted, death systematized.

We smoke and talk about nothing,
or what would persuade our future selves
into the cavernous despair of velour car seats,
or tie our hair up and read newspapers like our mothers.

A fishing hut is a place for logic and reason,
process, order and such, but you would die
at the roadside — destroyed, visceral,
gasping and gurgling. Glass would sparkle around you,

a maroon metal hood wounded, exposing
its shiny gears. An anarchy of conventional process,
you, a dead thing, would leave me gasping,
for a bucket, a hook. Heart plundered, hands lifted, gutted.

Beads and Blossoms

The old man from the porno store off Yonge Street
has been following us for two blocks.
His hands shook so much the oversize VHS box
nearly slipped away from him.

And now he has something to go home to,
I'm hoping — my squatting for the sick ones
wasn't lost on him, our laughter didn't go unnoticed,
that he can imagine us pissing champagne glasses full,
brimming with bitter fluids or spitting, swallowing,

whatever his preference — his wife cannot know.
But there are girls and girls on Carlton
who could tell you for a bill, force it aloofly beneath a bra strap,
lick their teeth free of gloss and get on with the evening.

That night, the parade, there were girls and there would be girls
for streets to come, drinking from coconuts, beads and blossoms
crying: *tits* — boys with Polaroids, boys with arms that stretched
green letters: *RIP*, *Lucy* or *Cold-blooded* — one had a snake,
    one a gold tooth.

Some time later I'll want to call you, remind you of this, whisper
    into the receiver
from a closet, maybe, a bathroom, so no husband or baby could
    identify the sounds.

Your First Affair

The damp midnight sickness
that shifts you from your side
of the bed to say *Let's never be
apart* — there will be no fierce,
depraved love for months.

We will lie like nations,
defeated, fearful, and you will
grasp at the blades of shoulders
and hair. Your first affair
is about virtue and truth.

But you will not know this until
the second: the lust and wilderness
of your discontent will leave you
scorned and lovely and more
charming than you've been in years.

God Does Not Love You Tonight

Drink beneath a panelled sky,
northern lights, and even the slaughterhouse
will charm and wink for you
in broken panes and chain-link fence.

What's churning, what roils
beyond the factory — not at day's break
or in our bloodless hours, behind door,
desk and key — what moves its violent hand

and makes a sky full, makes you sick
with hunger and desire, if not God?
You will wish there were a gentle organ
throbbing inaudibly for you, you will wish

you could hack out a rotten one: blistered
and pus-fattened, and forget lust and fervour
and even every great fuck you've had, not to feel
that hand, so weightless and promiscuous.

What father could be as silent as your own?
Does he know the ways you've tried
to love him or how you cast up both hands tonight
and asked for the burden of his touch?